I Decree....

Prayer Sniper

Audrena Crawford

To the men and women whose Faith in Jesus Christ made possible this inspiration in my life. To the men and women who was careless about my life. This book is gratefully and respectfully dedicated.

Contents

Chapter 1

The Light

I decree & I declare I shall not walk in darkness, I have the light of life. It is written, *"Then spake Jesus again unto them, saying, I am the light of the world: he that followeth me shall not walk in darkness, but shall have the light of life" (John 8:12 KJV).*

I decree & I declare I believe in Jesus therefore I will not abide in darkness. I find this promise when Jesus spoke it in John 12:46 (KJV), *"I am come a light into the world, that whosoever believeth on me should not abide in darkness."*

I decree & I declare I hear the voice of the LORD and I follow him. I will be given eternal life. I will never perish, no one will snatch me from the LORD'S hand. I find this promise when Jesus spoke it in John 10:27-29 (KJV), *"My sheep hear my voice, and I know them, and they follow me: And I give unto them eternal life; and they shall never perish, neither shall any man pluck them out of my hand. My father, which gave them me, is greater than all; and no man is able to pluck them out of my Father's hand."*

I decree & I declare the LORD my God will enlighten my darkness. It is written, *"For thou wilt light my candle: the LORD my God will enlighten my darkness"* (Psalm 18:28 KJV).

I decree & I declare my light is shining before others, they see my good works and they glorify my Father in heaven. In Matthew 5:16 Jesus says, *"Let your light so shine before men, that they may see your good works, and glorify your Father which is in heaven."*

I decree & I declare as my eye is the lamp of my body, my eye is single and my whole body is full of light. In Matthew 6:22 Jesus says, *"The light of the body is the eye: if therefore thine eye be single, thy whole body shall be full of light."*

Chapter 2

The Faithfulness

I decree & I declare my God is a faithful God, he keeps covenant with mercy for me because I love him and keep his commandments. It is written, *"Know therefore that the LORD thy God, he is God, the faithful God, which keepeth covenant and mercy with them that love him and keep his commandments to a thousand generations;"* (Deuteronomy 7:9 KJV).

I decree & I declare my God is a merciful God, he will not forsake me neither will he destroy me nor will he forget the covenant he made with me. It is written, *"(For the LORD thy God is a merciful God;) he will not forsake thee, neither destroy thee, nor forget the covenant of thy fathers which he sware unto them "*(Deuteronomy 4:31 KJV).

I decree & I declare even when I believe not, Jesus is faithful, he cannot deny himself. I am one with Jesus. Scripture states, *"If we believe not, yet he abideth faithful: he cannot deny himself "* (2 Timothy 2:13 KJV). In John 14:6 Jesus says, *"Abide in me, and I in you. As the branch cannot bear fruit of itself, except it abide in the vine; no more can ye, except ye abide in me."*

I decree & I declare my God will not break his covenant with me neither alter the thing that has come out of his lips concerning me. In Psalm 89:34 (KJV) God says, *"My covenant will I not break, nor alter the thing that is gone out of my lips."*

I decree & I declare I am blessed with forgiveness from my heavenly Father because I forgive men their trespasses. I find this promise spoken by Jesus in Matthew 6:14 (KJV),"For if ye forgive men their trespasses, your heavenly Father will also forgive you:"

I decree & I declare God who did not spare his own son is freely giving me all things that is good for me. It is written,*"He that spared not his own Son, but delivereth him up for us all, how shall he not with him also freely give us all things?"* (Romans 8:32 KJV).

I decree & I declare the Spirit of Truth, the Ruach HaKodesh, the blessed Holy Spirit is here to teach me all things and bring to my remembrance all that Jesus said to me. As Jesus said to Judas, not Judas Iscariot, *"But the Comforter, which is the Holy Ghost, whom the Father will send in my name, he shall teach you all things, and bring all things to your remembrance, whatsoever I have said unto you"* (John 14:26 KJV).

I decree & I declare the Helper, the Ruach HaKodesh,

the blessed Holy Spirit is helping me in my weakness, making intercession for me with groans that is too deep for words. It is written, *"Likewise the Spirit also helpeth our infirmities: for we know not what we should pray for as we ought: but the Spirit itself maketh intercession for us with groanings which cannot be uttered"* (Romans 8:26 KJV).

I decree & I declare the Comforter, the Ruach HaKodesh, the blessed Holy Spirit is upon me to be witnesses of Jesus & to walk in his power. In John 15:26 (KJV) Jesus says, *"But when the Comforter is come, whom I will send unto you from the Father, even the Spirit of truth, which proceedeth from the Father, he shall testify of me:"* and in Luke 10:19 (KJV) Jesus says, *"Behold, I give unto you power to tread on serpents and scorpions, and over all the power of the enemy: and nothing shall by any means hurt you."*

I decree & I declare everything I need shall be added unto me because I seek first the Kingdom of God and his righteousness. I find this promise where Jesus spoke it in Matthew 6:33 (KJV), *"But seek ye first the kingdom of God, and his righteousness; and all these things shall be added unto you."*

I decree & I declare I am pleasing to God & approved of men because I serve Christ in righteousness, peace and joy in the Holy Spirit. It is written, *"For the kingdom of God is not meat and drink; but righteousness, and peace, and joy in the Holy Ghost. For he that in these things serveth Christ is acceptable to God, and approved of men"* (Romans 14:17-18 KJV).

I decree & I declare I have the keys to the Kingdom of Heaven, whatever I bind on this earth is bound in heaven and whatever I loose on this earth is loosed in heaven. In Matthew 16:19 Jesus says, *"And I will give unto thee the keys of the kingdom of heaven: and whatsoever thou shalt bind on earth shall be bound in heaven: and whatsoever thou shalt loose on earth shall be loosed in heaven."*

I decree & I declare I am no longer a slave to sin; my old self is crucified with Jesus. My body is not ruled by sin. It is written, *"Being then made free from sin, ye became the servants of righteousness"* (Romans 6:18 KJV) and *"Let not sin therefore reign in your mortal body, that ye should obey it in the lusts thereof"* (Romans 6:12 KJV).

I decree & I declare I have a living hope by the resurrection of Jesus Christ from the dead. It is written, *"Blessed be the God and Father of our Lord Jesus Christ, which according to his abundant mercy hath begotten us again unto a lively hope by the resurrection of Jesus Christ from the dead"* (1 Peter 1:3 KJV).

I decree & I declare the Holy Spirit is bearing witness that I am a child of God. It is written, *"The Spirit itself beareth witness with our spirit, that we are the children of God:"* (Romans 8:16 KJV).

I decree & I declare I have the mind of Christ. It is written, *"For who hath known the mind of the Lord, that he may instruct him? but we have the mind of Christ"* (1 Corinthians 2:16 KJV).

I decree & I declare the Holy Spirit is manifested in me with the fruit of the spirit, love, joy, peace, longsuffering, gentleness, goodness, faith, meekness, and temperance. Everything contrary loses it's power over me. It is written, *" But the fruit of the Spirit is love, joy, peace, longsuffering, gentleness, goodness, faith, meekness, temperance: against such there is no law"* (Galatians 5:22-23 KJV).

Chapter 3

The Marriage

I decree & I declare me and my spouse will not be adulterers, whoremongers and our marriage bed is undefiled. It is written, *"Marriage is honourable in all, and the bed undefiled: but whoremongers and adulterers God will judge"* (Hebrews 13:4 KJV).

I decree & I declare my marriage is honorable, me and my spouse are called, justified and glorified. It is written, *"Moreover whom he did predestinate, them he also called: and whom he called, them he also justified: and whom he justified, them he also glorified"* (Romans 8:30 KJV).

I decree & I declare me and my spouse behold the beauty of the LORD, we dwell in his house and in the times of trouble we are hidden in his pavilion. In Psalm 27:4-5 it states, *"One thing have I desired of the LORD, that will I seek after; that I may dwell in the house of the LORD all the days of my life, to behold the beauty of the LORD, and to enquire in his temple. For in the time of trouble he shall hide me in his pavilion: in the secret of his tabernacle shall he hide me; he shall set me up upon a rock."*

I decree & I declare all of Satan devices are made

known to me and my spouse. It is made powerless and disarmed by the blood of Jesus. It is written, *"Lest Satan should get an advantage of us: for we are not ignorant of his devices"* (2 Corinthians 2:11 KJV).

I decree & I declare me and my spouse mind is on things above. Our life is not exposed but hidden with Christ in God. It is written, *"For ye are dead, and your life is hid with Christ in God"* (Colossians 3:3 KJV).

I decree & I declare my marriage is being held together by the LORD who is before all things, and by him all things consist. It is written, *"And he is before all things, and in him all things hold together"* (Colossians 1:17 KJV).

I decree & I declare I am fruitful & I multiply and fill the earth, subduing it with dominion over the fish of the sea, birds of the heaven and every living thing that moves on the earth. I find this blessing in Genesis 1:28 KJV, *"And God blessed them, and God said unto them, Be fruitful, and multiply, and have dominion over the fish of the sea, and over the fowl of the air, and over every living thing that moveth upon the earth."*

I decree & I declare me and my spouse have a bond of perfection because we put on love. We have a bond of peace and unity. It is written, *"But above all these things put on love, which is the bond of perfection"* (Colossians 3:14 NKJV).

I decree & I declare me and my spouse submits to one another out of reverence to Christ. It is written, *"Submitting yourselves one to another in the fear of God"* (Ephesians 5:21 KJV).

I decree & I declare me and my spouse is kind, tender hearted, forgiving one another as Christ forgave us. It is written, *"And be ye kind one to another, tenderhearted, forgiving one another, even as God for Christ's sake hath forgiven you"* (Ephesians 4:32 KJV).

Declarations for future spouse

I decree & I declare me and my future spouse control our body in sanctification and honor. It is written, *"For this is the will of God, even your sanctification, that ye should abstain from fornication: That every one of you should know how to possess his vessel in sanctification and honour;"* (1 Thessalonians 4:3-4).

*Declarations For Wives *

I decree & I declare my husband loves me and is not harsh, nor bitter with me.It is written, *"Husbands, love your wives, and be not bitter against them"* (Colossians 3:19 KJV).

I decree & I declare my husband lives with me in an understanding way, showing honour to me. It is written, *"Likewise, ye husbands, dwell with them according to knowledge, giving honour unto the wife, as unto the weaker vessel, and as being heirs together of the grace of life; that your prayers be not hindered"* (1 Peter 3:7 KJV).

I decree & I declare my husband loves me as Christ loves the church. It is written, *"Husbands, love your wives,even as Christ also loved the church, and gave himself for it;"* (Ephesians 5:25 KJV).

I decree & I declare my husband provides for me and the members of my household. It is written, *"But if any provide not for his own, and specially for those of his own house, he hath denied the faith, and is worse than an infidel"* (1 Timothy 5:8 KJV).

I decree & I declare my husband cleave to me his one flesh. It is written, *"Therefore shall a man leave his father and his mother, and shall cleave unto his wife: and they shall be one flesh"* (Genesis 2:24 KJV).

I decree & I declare the head of my husband is Jesus Christ and he is a good head over him. Scripture states, *"But I would have you know, that the head of every man is Christ; and the head of the woman is the man; and the head of Christ is God"* (1 Corinthians 11:3 KJV).

I decree & I declare my husband loves me as himself & I reverence my husband. It is written,

"Nevertheless let every one of you in particular so love his wife even as himself; and the wife see that she reverence her husband" (Ephesians 5:33 KJV).

I decree & I declare my husband doesn't look at women in a lustful intent, he escapes committing adultery in his heart. It is written, *"But I say unto you, That whosoever looketh on a woman to lust after her hath committed adultery with her already in his heart"* (Matthew 5:28 KJV).

I decree & I declare my husband doesn't provoke me to sin. It is written, *"Let us not therefore judge one another any more: but judge this rather, that no man put a stumblingblock or an occasion to fall in his brother's way"* (Romans 14:13 KJV).

I decree & I declare I am discreet, a keeper of my home, good, obedient to my husband so that the word of God be not blasphemed. It is written, *"To be discreet, chaste, keepers at home, good, obedient to their own husbands, that the word of God be not blasphemed"* (Titus 2:5 KJV).

I decree & I declare I am an excellent wife and a crown to my husband. It is written, *"A virtuous woman is a crown to her husband: but she that maketh ashamed is as rottenness in his bones"* (Proverbs 12:4 KJV).

Chapter 4

The Guidance

I decree & I declare my steps are ordered by the LORD, my step are ordered by his word and iniquity has no dominion over me. In Psalm 119:133 (KJV) it states, *"Order my steps on thy word: and let not any iniquity have dominion over me."*

I decree & I declare I acknowledge the LORD in all my ways and he shall direct my paths. It is written, *"In all thy ways acknowledge him, and he shall direct thy paths"* (Proverbs 3:6 KJV).

I decree & I declare the crooked things are made straight on my path. Just like the LORD said to his anointed *"I will go before thee, and make the crooked places straight: I will break in pieces the gates of brass, and cut in sunder the bars of iron:"* (Isaiah 45:2 KJV).

I decree & I declare the LORD himself is my wonderful counselor. It is written, *"For unto us a child is born, unto us a son is given, and the government will be upon his shoulders. And He will be called Wonderful Counselor, Mighty God, Everlasting Father, Prince of Peace"* (Isaiah 9:6 KJV).

I decree & I declare just as the universe was formed at God's command, everything I need for life and Godliness is formed by God's command and is released to me now. It is written, *"Through faith we understand that the worlds were framed by the word of God, so that things which are seen were not made of things which do appear"* (Hebrews 11:3 KJV).

I decree & I declare I have wisdom and the eyes of my understanding is enlightened. It is written , *"The eyes of your understanding being enlightened; that ye may know what is the hope of his calling, and what the riches of the glory of his inheritance in the saints,"* (Ephesians 1:18 KJV).

I decree & I declare the LORD perfect that which concerns me, he will not forsake the work of his hands just as David said in Psalm 138:8 (KJV), *"The LORD will perfect that which concerneth me: thy mercy, O LORD, endureth for ever: forsake not the works of thine own hands."*

I decree & I declare I am not conformed to this world; I am transformed by the renewal of my mind, I discern what is the good, acceptable & perfect will of God. It is written, *"And be not conformed to this world: but be ye transformed by the renewing of your mind, that ye may prove what is that good, and acceptable, and perfect, will of God"* (Romans 12:2 KJV).

I decree & I declare I think on whatever is true, noble, right, pure, lovely, admirable, praiseworthy and every thought that exalt itself against the knowledge of God is taken captive & brought to obedience to Christ Jesus. It is written, *"Finally, brethren, whatsoever things are true, whatsoever things are honest, whatsoever things are just, whatsoever things are pure, whatsoever things are lovely, whatsoever things are of good report; if there be any virtue, and if there be any praise, think on these things"* (Philippians 4:8 KJV).

I decree & I declare I trust in the LORD with all my heart and don't lean on my own understanding. It is written, *"Trust in the LORD with all thine heart; and lean not unto thine own understanding"* (Proverbs 3:5 KJV).

I decree & I declare nothing in all creation is hidden from God's sight, its uncovered and exposed before his eyes therefore he is causing me to escape evils, harm, danger, calamity, disaster, destruction. It is written, *"Neither is there any creature that is not manifest in his sight: but all things are naked and opened unto the eyes of him with whom we have to do"* (Hebrews 4:13 KJV).

I decree & I declare as I fear God, the secret of the LORD is with me & his covenant is revealed to me. It is written, *"The secret of the LORD is with them that fear him; and he will shew them his covenant"* (Psalm 25:14 KJV).

I decree & I declare the Holy Spirit is here with gifts, miracles, deliverance, prophecy, conviction, boldness, tongues of fire, to help me interpret spiritual things, to pour into my heart the love of God, to speak different languages by the Holy Spirit. It is written, *"And hope maketh not ashamed; because the love of God is shed abroad in our hearts by the Holy Ghost which is give unto us"* (Romans 5:5 KJV). It is written, *"Which things also we speak, not in the words which man's wisdom teacheth, but which the Holy Ghost teacheth; comparing spiritual things with spiritual"* (1 Corithians 2:13 KJV).

Chapter 5

The Blood

I decree & I declare I am reconciled to God because Jesus made peace through the blood of his cross. It is written, *"And, having made peace through the blood of his cross, by him to reconcile all things unto himself; by him, I say, whether they be things in earth, or things in heaven"* (Colossians 1:20 KJV).

I decree & I declare I am redeemed because of Jesus blood. My sins are forgiven in accordance with the riches of his grace. It is written, *"In whom we have redemption through his blood, the forgiveness of sins, according to the riches of his grace;"* (Ephesians 1:7 KJV).

I decree & I declare I have the confidence to enter the most Holy place because of the blood of Jesus. It is written, *"Having therefore, brethren, boldness to enter into the holiest by the blood of Jesus"* (Hebrews 10:19 KJV).

I decree & I declare I have been justified because

of Jesus blood and will be saved from God's wrath through Jesus. It is written, *"Much more then, being now justified by his blood, we shall be saved from wrath through him"* (Romans 5:9 KJV).

I decree & I declare I walk in the light and fellowship with Jesus and his blood cleans me from all sin. It is written, *"If we say that we have fellowship with him, and walk in darkness, we lie, and do not the truth: but if we walk in the light, we have fellowship one with another, and the blood of Jesus Christ his Son cleanseth us from all sin"* (1 John 1:6-7 KJV).

I decree & I declare Jesus is quickening me together with him, forgiven me of all trespasses, blotting out the handwriting of ordinances that is against me, which is contrary to me, taking it out of the way as it is already nailed to his cross, principalities & powers of darkness spoiled but I am victorious with Christ. It is written, *"And you, being dead in your sins and the uncircumcision of your flesh, hath he made quickened together with him, having forgiven you all trespasses; Blotting out the handwriting of ordinances that was against us, which was contrary to us, and took it out of the way, nailing it to his cross;"* (Colossians 2:13-14 KJV).

I decree & I declare Jesus suffered once for my sins to bring me to God. It is written, *"For Christ also hath once suffered for sins, the just for the unjust, that he might bring us to God, being put to death in the flesh, but quickened by the Spirit:"* (1 Peter 3:18 KJV).

I decree & I declare the blood of Jesus over my body, I am an honorable vessel. It is written, *"Therefore if anyone cleanses himself from the latter, he shall be a vessel for honor, sanctified, useful to the the Master, prepared for every good work"* (2 Timothy 2:21 KJV).

Chapter 6

The Judgment

I decree & I declare Jesus bare my sin and make intercession for my transgression. It is written, *"Therefore will I divide him a portion with the great, and he shall divide the spoil with the strong; because he hath poured out his soul unto death: and he was numbered with the transgressors; and he bare the sin of many, and made intercession for the transgressors"* (Isaiah 53:12 KJV).

I decree & I declare Kingship belongs to the LORD and he is ruling over my city, my state, my nation. It is written, *"All the ends of the world shall remember and turn to the LORD: and all the kindreds of the nations shall worship before thee. For the kingdom is the LORD'S: and he is the governor among the nations"* (Psalm 22:27-28 KJV)

I decree & I declare I am no longer a slave to those who by nature are not gods because I am now known by God and know him therefore the weak and worthless principles have no hold on me. It is written, *"Howbeit then, when ye knew not God, ye did service unto them which by nature are no gods. But now, after that ye have known God, or rather are known of God, how turn ye again to the weak and beggarly elements, whereunto ye desire again to be in bondage?"* (Galatians 4:9 KJV).

I decree & I declare I am a royal priesthood and my house is filled with the glory of God. Just like the glory filled the house of God in 2 Chronicles 5:14 (KJV) *"So that the priests could not stand to minister by reason of the cloud: for the glory of the LORD had filled the house of God."* It is written, *"But ye are a chosen generation, a royal priesthood, an holy nation, a peculiar people; that ye should shew forth the praises of him who hath called you out of darkness into his marvellous light"* (1 Peter 2:9 KJV).

I decree & I declare every demon spirit causing agitation, chaos, disarray and disorder is casted out from my midst just as Jesus commanded his disciples to cast out devils. It is written, *"Heal the sick, cleanse the lepers, raise the dead, cast out devils: freely ye have received, freely give"* (Matthew 10:8 KJV).

I decree & I declare Jesus has given me the glory that the Father gave him so that I am one with Jesus like he is one with the Father just like he did for his disciples. It is written, *"And the glory which thou gavest me I have given them; that they may be one, even as we are one:"* (John 17:22 KJV).

I decree & I declare I am perfectly united to Christ Jesus so the world may know that Jesus loves me just like he did for his disciples. It is written, *"I in them, and thou in me, that they may be made perfect in one; and that the world may know that thou hast sent me, and hast loved them, as thou hast loved me"* (John 17:23 KJV).

I decree & I declare the divine power of God has granted me all things that pertain to life and Godliness. It is written, *"According as his divine power hath given us all things that pertain unto life and godliness, through the knowledge of him that hath called us to glory and virtue:"* (2 Peter 1:3 KJV).

I decree & I declare love has been perfected among me so that I have confidence on the day of Judgment for in this world I am just like Jesus. It is written, *"Herein is our love made perfect, that we may have boldness in the day of judgment: because as he is, so are we in this world"* (1 John 4:17 KJV).

I decree & I declare angels of the LORD is given charge over me to keep me in all thy ways, to bear me up in their hands, so I don't dash my foot against a stone just as it is stated in Psalm 91:11-12 (KJV), *"For he shall give his angels charge over thee, to keep thee in all thy ways. They shall bear thee up in their hands, lest thou dash thy foot against a stone."*

I decree & I declare the prince of this world has been casted out of my midst. *"Now is the judgment of this world: now shall the prince of this world be cast out. And I, if I be lifted up from the earth, will draw all men unto me"* (John 12:32 KJV).

I decree & I declare the prince of this world is condemned . It is written, *"Of Judgment, because the prince of this world is judged"* (John 16:11 KJV).

I decree & I declare Jesus is at the right hand of God, with Angels, authorities and powers made subject to him therefore no power of the enemy shall prevail against me. It is written, *"Who is gone into heaven, and is on the right hand of God; angels and authorities and powers being made subject unto him"* (1 Peter 3:22 KJV).

I decree & I declare all things were created in heaven and on earth by God and for God, rather it is visible or invisible, rather it is thrones, powers, rulers, or authorities, they are created by God and for God. It is written, *"For by him were all things created, that are in heaven, and that are in earth, visible and invisible, whether they be thrones, or dominion, or principalities, or powers: all things were created by him, and for him:"* (Colossians 1:16 KJV).

I decree & I declare Jesus declare to me the name of the Father and the love which the Father has for Jesus is in me. It is written, *"And I have declared unto them thy name, and will declare it: that the love wherewith thou hast loved me may be in them, and I in them"* (John 17:26 KJV).

I decree & I declare Jesus has prepared a place for me and he will come back to welcome me into his presence so that I may be where he is. It is written, *"And If I go and prepare a place for you, I will come again, and receive you unto myself; that where I am, there ye may be also"* (John 14:3 KJV).

I decree & I declare I serve Jesus and the Father himself is honoring me. In John 12:26 Jesus says, *"If any man serve me, let him follow me; and where I am, there shall also my servant be: if any man serve me, him will my Father honour."*

I decree & I declare where Jesus is seated so am I seated in heavenly places with him. It is written, *"And hath raised us up together, and made us sit together in heavenly places in Christ Jesus:"* (Ephesians 2:6 KJV).

I decree & I declare I will see the glory the Father gave to Jesus. It is written, *"Father, I will that they also, whom thou hast given me, be with me where I am; that they may behold my glory, which thou hast given me: for thou lovedst me before the foundation of the world"* (John 17:24 KJV).

I decree & I declare as I come to Jesus he will never turn me away. It is written, *"All that the Father gives me shall comes to me; and him that cometh to me I will in no wise cast out"* (John 6:37 KJV).

I decree & I declare God bestows wealth on me because I love wisdom and he makes my treasures full. It is written, *"I lead in the way of righteousness, in the midst of the paths of judgment: That I may cause those that love me to inherit substance; and I will fill their treasures"* (Proverbs 8:21 KJV).

I decree & I declare the blessings of the LORD enrich my life and he add no sorrow to it. It is written, *"The blessing of the LORD, it maketh rich, and he addeth no sorrow with it"* (Proverbs 10:22 KJV).

I decree & I declare Jesus gave himself for me to redeem me from all lawlessness, to purify me for himself. I shall be zealous for good deeds. It is written, *"Who gave himself for us, that he might redeem us from all iniquity, and purify unto himself a peculiar people, zealous for good deeds"* (Titus 2:14 KJV).

I decree & I declare as my ways are pleasing to the LORD he is making my enemies seek peace with me. It is written, *"When a man's ways please the LORD, he maketh even his enemies to be at peace with him"* (Proverbs 16:7 KJV).

I decree & I declare I am delivered out of the hands of my enemies and I serve God without fear according to the oath he swore to our father Abraham. It is written, *"That he would grant unto us, that we being delivered out of the hand of our enemies might serve him without fear, in holiness and righteousness before him, all the days of our life"* (Luke 1:74-75 KJV).

I decree & I declare I keep watch and pray always that I may be accounted worthy to escape all the things that shall come to pass so those days don't come upon me like a trap. I shall be able to stand before the Son of man and stand before him blameless.It is written, *"Watch ye therefore, and pray always, that ye may be accounted worthy to escape all these things that shall come to pass and to stand before the Son of man"* **(Luke 21:36 KJV).**

Chapter 7

The Vengeance

I decree & I declare I love my enemies. I bless those that curse me. I do good to those who hate me. I pray for those who despitefully use and persecute me because I am a child of my Father who is in heaven. It is written, *"But I say unto you, Love your enemies, bless them that curse you, do good to them that hate you, and pray for them which despitefully use you, and persecute you; that ye may be the children of your Father which is in heaven: for he maketh his sun to rise on the evil and on the good, and sendeth rain on the just and on the unjust"* (Matthew 5:44-45 KJV).

I decree & I declare everyone who is evil and hurtful towards me will be overwhelmed with the love of God and visited by Jesus. It is written, *"And as he journeyed, he came near Damascus: and suddenly there shined round about him a light from heaven: And he fell to the earth, and heard a voice saying unto him, Saul, Saul, why persecutest thou me?"* (Acts 9:3-4 KJV).

I decree & I declare I am merciful just as the Father in heaven is merciful. I do not judge, I do not condemn, I forgive. It is written, *"Be ye therefore merciful, as your Father also is merciful. Judge not, and ye shall not be judged: condemn not. and ye shall not be condemned: forgive, and ye shall be forgiven"* (Luke 6:36-37 KJV).

I decree & I declare the right hand of the LORD is glorious in power dashing into pieces the enemy. It is written, *"Thy right hand, O LORD, is become glorious in power: thy right hand , O LORD, hath dashed in pieces the enemy"* (Exodus 15:6 KJV).

I decree & I declare through God I shall do courageously and in an excellent way for it is he that is treading down my enemies. It is written, *" Through God we shall do valiantly: for he it is that shall tread down our enemies"* (Psalm 60:12 KJV).

I decree & I declare God is avenging the elect that cry day and night. It is written, *"And shall not God avenge his own elect, which cry day and night unto him, though he bear long with them?"* (Luke 18:7 KJV).

I decree & I declare the fire of God is consuming the works of the devil that is operating in me, in my house, in my children and in my family. Works of satan be destroyed, I say. It is written, *"He that committeth sin is of the devil; for the devil sinneth from the beginning. For this purpose the Son of God was manifested, that he might destroy the works of the devil"* (1 John 3:8 KJV).

Made in the USA
Middletown, DE
08 January 2023

21072306R00020